FINANCIAL FREEDOM

Everything You Need to Know

BB MYRDAL

ISBN-13: 9798866048779
ISBN-10: 1477123456

Cover design by: Art Painter
Library of Congress Control Number: 2018675309
Printed in the United States of America

CONTENTS

FOREWORD

Welcome to this book, your guide to achieving financial freedom. Inside, you'll find a comprehensive overview of what you need to learn and master on your journey.

I've kept things simple, with no lengthy explanations or extra stories. The material is presented concisely for a clear overall understanding.

You might notice some repetitions, intentionally to emphasize key points and ensure each chapter stands on its own.

Feel free to jump into any chapter without reading the whole book. Let's embark on this journey to financial freedom together.

BB MYRDAL

1. CHAPTER INTRODUCTION TO FINANCIAL FREEDOM

Financial freedom, an esteemed state, goes beyond mere monetary wealth, encompassing a holistic sense of autonomy and security. It is not only about having a certain amount of money; it's about having the financial resources to live the life you desire, make choices without constant worry about money, and have the flexibility to respond to opportunities or challenges. It's a journey that involves smart decision-making, strategic planning, and a mindset shift towards a life where one's financial resources align with personal aspirations. In this exploration of financial freedom, we uncover the principles, practices, and the profound impact that achieving financial autonomy can have on every aspect of your life.

a. Defining Financial Freedom

Financial freedom is the life situation where an individual can make choices about their life and pursue their goals without being overly constrained by financial constraints or obligations.

The Key Aspects Of Financial Freedom Include:

1. Sufficient Savings and Emergency Fund:

Financial freedom often starts with having savings and an emergency fund that can cover living expenses for a specified period, providing safety in unexpected situations.

2. Debt Management:

Being free from overwhelming debt is a crucial component of financial freedom. This includes not only minimizing high-interest debt but also having a plan to eliminate it.

3. Income Streams:

Financially free individuals often have multiple sources of income, which may include earned income, passive income from investments, and possibly income from side businesses or ventures.

4. Budgeting and Spending Control:

Understanding and managing one's budget is fundamental. Financial freedom involves being mindful of spending, budgeting effectively, and avoiding unnecessary debt.

5. Investing for the Future:

Investing is a key element of financial freedom. It involves making money work for you, potentially generating passive income, and providing for long-term financial goals such as retirement.

6. Ability to Pursue Personal Goals:

Ultimately, financial freedom is about having the financial means to pursue personal goals, whether they involve travel, education, entrepreneurship, or any other aspirations.

* * *

Keep in mind that financial freedom is a subjective concept, and what it means can vary from person to person. It's about aligning one's financial resources with their values and life objectives, allowing for a sense of security, choice, and fulfilment.

b.　Why Financial Freedom Matters

Financial freedom matters for several significant reasons, impacting various aspects of an individual's life. It is about gaining control over one's financial situation and using that control to live a life aligned with personal values and aspirations. Financial freedom empowers individuals to take charge of their circumstances, aligning their lives with values and aspirations beyond mere wealth accumulation.

The Main Reasons Why Financial Freedom Truly Matters:

1.　Flexibility and Choices:

Financial freedom provides individuals with the flexibility to make choices based on personal preferences rather than financial constraints. This could include choices about career paths, lifestyle, and how time is spent.

2.　Reduced Stress and Anxiety:

Dealing with financial problems can cause a lot of stress and anxiety. Achieving financial freedom can alleviate these pressures, leading to better mental health and an improved overall sense of well-being.

3.　Quality of Life:

Financial freedom directly contributes to an improved quality of life. It allows individuals to afford the things that matter to them, whether that's quality housing, education, travel, or leisure activities.

4.　Security and Stability:

Financial freedom provides a safety net, offering security and stability. With sufficient savings and a well-managed financial plan, individuals are better equipped to handle unexpected expenses, job losses, or economic downturns.

5. Personal Growth and Pursuit of Passion:

When financial concerns are minimized, individuals can focus on personal growth and pursue their passions. This might involve investing time and resources in hobbies, education, or entrepreneurial endeavours.

6. Generational Impact:

Financial freedom enables individuals to leave a positive financial legacy for their children and future generations. This might involve funding education, providing financial assistance, or leaving an inheritance.

7. Retirement Comfort:

Financial freedom is closely linked to a comfortable retirement. With careful financial planning and savings, individuals can retire with confidence, enjoying their later years without financial worries.

8. Empowerment and Independence:

Financial freedom empowers individuals to take control of their lives. It reduces dependency on others and fosters a sense of independence and self-reliance.

9. Philanthropy and Giving Back:

Financial freedom allows individuals to contribute to charitable causes and give back to the community. This sense of philanthropy can bring a deep sense of fulfilment and purpose.

10. Freedom to Explore Opportunities:

Financially free individuals have the flexibility to explore new opportunities, whether in their careers or personal lives. This could involve starting a business, pursuing further education, or taking on new challenges.

* * *

Financial freedom is about having the freedom to live life on one's terms, unencumbered by financial constraints, and with the ability to pursue personal goals and aspirations.

2. CHAPTER   ASSESSING YOUR FINANCIAL HEALTH

Budgeting and expense tracking are fundamental financial management practices that play a crucial role in achieving financial freedom and ensuring long-term financial stability. By diligently budgeting and tracking expenses, individuals gain a clear understanding of their financial landscape, make informed decisions, and pave the way toward achieving the coveted goal of financial freedom.

a. Budgeting

Budgeting involves developing a plan that details how you will distribute your income to meet your expenses and reach your financial objectives. It's a roadmap for managing your money and ensuring that you live within your means.

Here Are The Key Components Of Budgeting:

1. Income

Identify and list all sources of income, including salary, bonuses, freelance work, or any other money coming in.

2. Expenses

Categorize your expenses into fixed (consistent monthly bills like rent, mortgage, utilities) and variable (expenses that may vary, like groceries, entertainment, dining out).

3. Savings and Investments

Allocate a part of your budget for savings and investments. This includes emergency funds, retirement accounts, and other long-term savings goals, and is important for building a financial cushion, preparing for the future, and achieving your desired financial milestones.

4. Debt Repayment

If you have outstanding debts, allocate a portion of your budget to debt repayment. This proactive step ensures that you are actively addressing your financial obligations and working towards reducing your overall debt burden, paving the way for financial freedom and a more secure financial future.

5. Miscellaneous Expenses

Additional tips for budgeting:

- Be realistic about your income and expenses.
- Review and adjust your budget regularly, especially if there are changes in your financial situation.
- Prioritize needs over wants, especially if you're working towards specific financial goals.
- Use budgeting tools and apps to streamline the process and track spending.

Account for unexpected or irregular expenses. Having a miscellaneous category can help cover unforeseen costs.

❊ ❊ ❊

Regularly evaluating your financial health empowers you to pinpoint areas for enhancement and make informed choices to improve your overall financial well-being.

b.   Expense Tracking

Expense tracking involves monitoring and recording all your expenditures. This practice gives you an overview of where your money is going and ensures that the expenses stay within the limits set by your budget.

Here Are The Key Components Of Expense Tracking:

1.   Record Every Expense

Keep a detailed record of all your expenditures, no matter how small. This includes cash transactions, credit card purchases, and electronic transactions. Keeping your expenses recorded enables a clear understanding of spending patterns and facilitates informed financial decision-making.

2.   Categorize Expenses

Assign categories to your expenses, such as groceries, entertainment, transportation, and utilities. An organized approach allows you to identify areas where you may have overspent or have opportunities to save, contributing to a more informed and controlled financial management strategy.

3.   Compare Actual Spending to Budget

Regularly compare your actual spending to your budget. This gives you information about where you may be overspending or where adjustments to your budget are necessary.

4.   Identify Trends

Over time, expense tracking can help you identify trends

in your spending behaviour. This awareness is crucial for making informed financial decisions and changing behaviour to better align with your financial goals.

Additional tips for expense tracking:

- Use expense-tracking apps or software to automate the process.
- Keep all receipts or make use of digital receipts.
- Regularly review your spending patterns to identify areas for improvement.
- Be honest and thorough in recording all expenses.

---

* * *

By combining budgeting and expense tracking, you can gain better control over your finances, make informed decisions, and work towards the goal of financial freedom. These practices provide the foundation for wise financial management and the ability to allocate resources effectively.

c. Evaluating Your Current Financial Situation

Evaluating your current financial situation is a crucial step in the path towards financial freedom. This important process involves a comprehensive review of your income, expenses, assets, and liabilities, providing a deep and clear understanding of your financial standing, which is crucial for all further financial planning and goal setting.

Here's A Guide On How To Evaluate Your Financial Situation:

1. Create a List of Income Sources:

List all your sources of income, including your salary, bonuses, freelance or side gig income, rental income, dividends, and any other sources. Be accurate and don´t leave any stone unturned.

2. Assess Your Monthly Expenses:

Create a detailed breakdown of your monthly expenses. Organize them into fixed costs (rent or mortgage, utilities, insurance etc.) and variable expenses (groceries, dining out, entertainment etc.). Again, be accurate and don´t leave any stone unturned.

3. Calculate Your Net Income:

Subtract your total monthly expenses from your total monthly income to determine your net income. A positive net income indicates that you are living within your means.

4. Analyze Your Debt Situation:

List all your debts, including credit cards, mortgages, car

and student loans, loans from family and friends etc. Take note of the interest rates and monthly payments associated with each.

5. Calculate Your Net Worth:

Subtract your total liabilities (debts) from your total assets (savings, investments, property). This calculation provides an overview of your overall financial health, providing crucial information about your current standing.

6. Review Your Emergency Fund:

Assess the adequacy of your emergency fund. Financial experts often recommend having three to six months' worth of living expenses saved in an easily accessible account.

7. Examine Your Investment Portfolio:

If you have investments, review their performance, and assess whether your portfolio aligns with your financial goals and risk tolerance.

8. Evaluate Your Insurance Coverage:

Review your insurance policies, including health, life, property, and any other coverage. Ensure that your coverage meets your current needs but at the same time is not too much or unnecessary.

9. Check Your Credit Report:

Obtain a copy of your credit report and check for inaccuracies. A good credit score is important for various financial transactions and can impact your ability to borrow on favourable terms.

10. Assess Your Financial Goals:

Revisit your financial goals and assess your progress

towards achieving them. Adjust your goals, if necessary, based on changes in your life or priorities.

11. Consider Your Retirement Savings:

Review your retirement savings accounts and assess whether your contributions align with your retirement goals.

* * *

Regularly reassessing your financial situation is key to adapting to life changes and staying on track towards financial freedom. It allows you to make informed decisions, identify areas for improvement, and ensure that your financial goals remain realistic and achievable.

3. CHAPTER SETTING FINANCIAL GOALS

Setting financial goals is crucial for your financial well-being. When setting financial goals, applying the SMART criteria can enhance clarity and increase the likelihood of success. Prioritize short-term and long-term goals for effective financial planning and well-being.

a.   SMART Goal Setting

SMART is an acronym that stands for Specific, Measurable, Achievable, Relevant, and Time-bound. It is well known for all kinds of goal setting and can be very useful for financial goal setting. This method aids in maintaining focus on your achievements, providing a clear, measurable, and achievable vision for reaching your goals. By eliminating distractions along the way, it facilitates a more straightforward path to success.

Here's A Breakdown Of Each Element For Smart Goal Setting:

1. Specific

Specify your goals instead of being vague. Rather than saying "Save money," be clear, like "Save $3,000 for an emergency fund within the next 18 months."

For specific goals, answer key questions like who, what, where, when and why, making it easier to focus and track progress.

2. Measurable

Rather than saying "Pay off debt," make it measurable like "Pay off $12,000 in credit card debt by making monthly payments of $900."

Measurable goals allow you to monitor progress and establish when you've successfully achieved the goal. It provides a way to assess your journey and stay motivated.

3. Achievable

Make sure your goal is realistic and achievable within your current circumstances. Instead of aiming to save $12,000 in three months on a $45,000 annual income, set a goal that aligns with your financial capacity.

Goals should stretch you but also be realistic. An achievable goal is challenging yet possible with effort and commitment.

4. Relevant

Align financial goals with broader life objectives. For example, if buying a home is a long-term goal, focus on saving for a down payment.

Relevant goals tie into overall priorities, ensuring you're working toward something meaningful.

5. Time-bound

Make your goal specific and time-bound. Instead of "Save for retirement," say "Contribute $400 monthly to my retirement account for the next 30 years.".

A timeframe adds urgency, prevents procrastination, and provides a clear deadline to stay on track.

Additional tips for goal setting:

- **Break Down Larger Goals**:
- If your ultimate financial goal is substantial, break it down into smaller, more manageable milestones. This makes the goal-setting process less overwhelming.
- **Regularly Review and Adjust:**
- Life circumstances can change. Regularly review your goals, assess progress, and adjust as needed. Be flexible, especially if unexpected events occur.
- **Celebrate Achievements:**
  When you reach a milestone or achieve a goal, celebrate your success. Noticing how far you have come can boost motivation and help you stick to good money habits.

* * *

Applying the SMART framework to your financial goals provides a structured and strategic approach, increasing the likelihood of successful implementation and attainment of your goals within a certain time frame.

b. Prioritizing Short-term and Long-term Goals

Prioritizing short-term and long-term financial goals is essential for effective financial planning and balance. Maintaining this balance goes beyond mere month-to-month survival. A robust financial strategy involves consistently budgeting for expenses to guarantee an ample reserve of cash, particularly in periods of economic uncertainty.

Here's A Guide On How To Prioritize These Goals:

1. Identify Your Goals:

Make a list of both short-term and long-term financial goals. Short-term goals might involve establishing an emergency fund, repaying debt, or saving for a dream car. Long-term objectives might involve acquiring a home, financing kids' education, or preparing for retirement.

2. Categorize Goals:

Separate your goals into categories. Common categories include emergency fund, debt repayment, education, homeownership, retirement, and other specific objectives you may have.

3. Evaluate Timeframes:

Determine the timeframes for each goal. Short-term goals typically have a timeline of one to three years, while long-term goals may span five years or more and often entail a more significant financial commitment.

4. Assess Financial Impact:

Consider the financial implications of each goal. Certain

goals may demand substantial financial resources, while others might have a more modest impact on your budget.

5. Consider Interest Rates:

When managing outstanding debts, it's crucial to consider the associated interest rates. High-interest debts, like those from credit cards, should be prioritized due to the substantial financial strain they can impose. Addressing these debts promptly can alleviate significant financial pressure.

6. Emergency Fund as a Priority:

Establishing an emergency fund is usually a priority. Having a financial safety net can prevent the need to go into debt in case of unexpected expenses.

7. Balance Your Portfolio of Goals:

Aim for a balanced approach. While certain goals may be more pressing, it's important to allocate some resources to longer-term objectives to benefit from compounding over time.

8. Align Goals with Values:

Consider the importance of each goal in relation to your values and lifestyle. Prioritize goals that match your core values and aspirations.

9. Risk Tolerance:

Assess your risk tolerance. Some goals may involve riskier investments, so understanding your comfort level with risk is crucial.

10. Review and Adjust Regularly:

Regularly review and adjust your priorities as

circumstances change. Life events, economic conditions, or personal goals may shift over time.

Example Prioritization:

High-Priority Short-Term Goals (1-3 years):
- Save up for an emergency fund.
- Pay off high-interest debt.
- Save for a specific upcoming expense (e.g., vacation, wedding).

Mid-Priority Goals (3-5 years):
- Save for a down payment on a home.
- Contribute to education funds.
- Start a retirement savings plan.

Long-Term Goals (5+ years):
- Maximize retirement contributions.
- Save for children's education.
- Invest in long-term wealth-building opportunities.

Additional tips for prioritizing:

- **Be Realistic:** Ensure that your goals are realistic and achievable given your current financial situation.
- **Create a Timeline:** Assign specific timelines to
- each goal. This creates a sense of urgency and helps with planning.
- **Seek Professional Advice:** If needed, consult with a financial advisor to get personalized guidance based on your unique circumstances.

* * *

By smartly placing importance on both immediate and future objectives, you can design a path for your financial journey that matches your values and dreams. Regularly reviewing and tweaking your priorities makes certain that your financial plan stays up-to-date and flexible.

4. CHAPTER CREATING A STRATEGIC FINANCIAL PLAN

Creating a strategic financial plan is crucial for intentional decision-making and securing your future. This chapter is divided into two essential sections: Building an Effective Budget, which empowers you to allocate resources wisely, and Establishing an Emergency Fund, providing a financial safety net for unexpected challenges, ensuring a comprehensive approach to financial well-being.

a. Building an Effective Budget

Building an effective budget is a foundational step toward financial stability and freedom. A well-crafted budget allows you to allocate your income wisely, save for the future, and achieve your financial goals.

Here's A Guide On How To Build An Effective Budget:

1. Gather Financial Information:

Collect information about your income, including your salary, bonuses, side hustle earnings, and any other sources of income. Gather details about your monthly expenses, including fixed bills, variable expenses, and discretionary spending.

2. Categorize Your Expenses:

Categorize all expenses into fixed and variable categories. Fixed expenses include rent or mortgage, utilities, loan payments, and insurance. Variable expenses include groceries, entertainment, and discretionary spending.

3. List Your Financial Goals:

Clearly define your financial objectives, encompassing both short-term and long-term goals. These may involve establishing an emergency fund, eliminating debt, saving for a vacation, or investing for retirement.

4. Determine Your Net Income:

Determine your net income by deducting your total monthly expenses from your total monthly income. If you are living within your means the net income will be positive, if not the outcome is negative.

5. Create a Zero-Based Budget:

Assign every dollar a specific purpose. Ensure that your income equals your expenses. This ensures that every dollar is allocated, whether it's for bills, savings, investments, or discretionary spending.

6. Prioritize Savings:

Allocate a portion of your income to savings as a non-negotiable expense. This includes contributions to your emergency fund, retirement accounts, and other savings goals.

7. Track Your Spending:

Regularly track your actual spending against your budget. Use tools like budgeting apps or spreadsheets to follow your expenditures. Examine areas that exhibit warning signs of overspending.

8. Adjust and Fine-Tune:

Be flexible with your budget. Life circumstances and unexpected expenses may arise. Consistently revisit and modify your budget to incorporate changes and ensure it remains realistic.

9. Eliminate or Reduce Unnecessary Expenses:

Spot areas where you can reduce your expenses. This might involve reducing discretionary spending, negotiating bills, or finding more cost-effective alternatives.

10. Plan for Irregular Expenses:

Anticipate and plan for irregular expenses, such as annual insurance premiums, taxes, or maintenance costs. Allocate a portion of your budget to cover these expenses when they arise.

11. Emergency Fund Contributions:

Prioritize building and maintaining an emergency fund. This fund serves as financial safety and helps avoid the necessity of resorting to credit cards or loans when faced with unforeseen expenses.

12. Review Regularly and Set Goals:

Regularly review your budget and financial goals. Celebrate achievements and adjust your budget to align with changing priorities.

Additional tips for building an effective budget:

- **Be Realistic:** Set realistic spending limits and savings goals. Unrealistic expectations can lead to frustration and make it challenging to stick to your budget.
- **Involve Family Members:** If applicable, involve family members or those sharing expenses in the budgeting process. It fosters cooperation and ensures that everyone is on the same page.
- **Use Technology:** Leverage budgeting apps and tools to streamline the process. Many apps can automatically categorize expenses and provide insights into your spending habits.

❊ ❊ ❊

Remember, a budget is a dynamic tool that evolves with your life and financial circumstances. Regularly revisiting and adjusting your budget ensures that it remains effective and aligned with your financial goals.

b. Establishing an Emergency Fund

Establishing an emergency fund is a crucial step in achieving financial stability and resilience. An emergency fund serves as a financial safety net, offering protection against unforeseen expenses or disruptions in income.

Here's A Guide On How To Establish And Manage An Emergency Fund:

1. Set a Target Amount:

Decide the amount on your emergency fund goal. A common guideline is three to six months' living expenses, but the suitable amount varies based on individual circumstances and risk tolerance.

2. Assess Your Living Expenses:

Calculate your monthly living expenses, including rent or mortgage, utilities, groceries, insurance, loan payments, and other necessities. Multiply this amount by the desired number of months to determine your target emergency fund amount. An emergency fund usually covers at least 3 to 6 months' worth of living expenses.

3. Start Small if Necessary:

If saving a full emergency fund seems daunting, start with a smaller, achievable goal, and gradually increase it over time. The key is to start building the habit of saving regularly.

4. Choose a Separate Account:

Emergency funds should be kept in a separate and easily accessible account. Consider a savings account or a money market account that offers liquidity while also earning some interest.

5. Automate Your Savings:

Set up automatic transfers to your emergency fund each time you receive income. Automation ensures that you consistently contribute to your fund, making saving a routine part of your financial habits.

6. Prioritize the Fund:

Treat your emergency fund as a priority. Allocate a portion of your budget specifically for emergency fund contributions. Consider it a non-negotiable expense that you cannot avoid.

7. Cut Unnecessary Expenses:

Pinpoint areas where reducing optional expenses is possible to increase your contributions to the emergency fund. This might involve reducing dining out, entertainment expenses, or other non-essential purchases.

8. Use Windfalls Wisely:

Allocate unexpected windfalls, such as tax refunds, bonuses, or gifts, to your emergency fund. This can significantly accelerate your progress and move you faster toward your goals.

9. Review and Adjust:

Regularly review your budget and assess whether you can increase your monthly contributions to the emergency fund. Adjust your contributions as your financial situation evolves.

10. Avoid Temptation:

Resist the temptation to dip into the fund for non-emergencies. Define what constitutes a true emergency (e.g., medical expenses, car repairs) to maintain the integrity of the fund.

11. Replenish After Use:

If you need to use your emergency fund for a legitimate emergency, make it a priority to replenish the fund as soon as possible.

12. Consider Interest Rates:

While accessibility is crucial, consider placing your emergency fund in an account that earns a reasonable interest rate. This way, your money works for you even in the fund.

13. Review and Adjust Over Time:

As your financial situation changes, reassess the adequacy of your emergency fund. Life changes, like switching jobs, getting married, or having a child, might require adjustments.

Additional tips for building an emergency fund:

- **Stay Consistent**: Consistency is key when building an emergency fund. Even small, regular contributions can add up over time.
- **Educate Family Members:** Ensure that family members are aware of the purpose of the emergency fund and the importance of not using it for non-emergencies.
- **Celebrate Milestones:** Celebrate reaching milestones in your emergency fund savings journey. It can be motivating and reinforce positive financial habits.

---

* * *

Building an emergency fund provides financial peace of mind and protects against the uncertainties of life. It's a foundational step toward achieving broader financial goals and establishing a solid financial foundation.

c. Managing Debt

Managing debt is a critical aspect of achieving financial stability and working towards financial freedom; it empowers individuals to regain control of their finances, reduce stress, and foster a secure financial future.

Here's A Comprehensive Guide On How To Effectively Manage Debt:

1. List Your Debts

Create a list of all your debts, such as mortgages, car loans, credit cards and student loans. Record the remaining balances, interest rates, and minimum monthly payments for each.

2. Prioritize High-Interest Debt

Rank your debts from highest to lowest interest and pay the highest rate of debt first. These debts, f. ex. credit card balances, often accumulate interest at a faster rate and can significantly impact your financial health.

3. Create a Debt Repayment Plan

Develop a plan for repaying debts, like the snowball (paying the smallest debts first) or avalanche method (tackling highest-interest debts first). Choose a strategy that suits your preferences and financial situation.

4. Set Realistic Goals

Establishing realistic and achievable goals for debt repayment is crucial. Breaking down larger goals into smaller, manageable milestones not only makes the process more feasible but also helps maintain motivation throughout the journey to financial freedom.

5. Review Your Budget

Review your budget to find places where you can reduce expenses and redirect more funds toward repaying your debts. Consider prioritizing debt payments over discretionary spending.

6. Negotiate Interest Rates

Reach out to your creditors to discuss and negotiate lower interest rates. Securing a reduced interest rate can substantially lessen the overall cost of repaying your debts.

7. Consolidate Debt Responsibly

Explore debt consolidation options, such as a personal loan or a balance transfer to a low-interest credit card. However, be cautious and ensure that the consolidation doesn't lead to further financial strain.

8. Build an Emergency Fund

Simultaneously work on building an emergency fund. Having a financial safety net can prevent the need to rely on credit cards or other loans when unexpected expenses arise.

9. Avoid Accumulating New Debt

Avoid new debt while repaying existing obligations. Use cash for purchases, resist new credit urges, and create a budget for spending guidance.

10. Professional Advice

If dealing with debt challenges, consider consulting a financial counsellor. Professionals can guide budgeting, negotiating with creditors, and developing a sustainable repayment plan.

11. Automate Payments

Set up automatic payments for your minimum monthly obligations to avoid late fees. This ensures that you stay current on your debts even during busy or challenging times.

12. Celebrate Milestones

Celebrate small victories along the way. Paying off a credit card or reaching a debt repayment milestone can be a significant achievement and a source of motivation.

13. Educate Yourself

Invest time in learning and understanding the terms and conditions of your loans. Understanding details such as interest rates, fees, and repayment options empowers you to make better decisions.

14. Consider Professional Help for Severe Cases

In severe cases of debt, bankruptcy might be a last resort. Consult with a bankruptcy attorney to explore your options and understand the potential implications.

Additional tips for managing debts:

- **Stay Persistent:** Debt repayment is a gradual process. Progress might seem slow at times, but it's crucial to stay persistent and committed.
- **Review and Adjust Your Plan:** Regularly review your debt repayment plan and adjust it. Life is dynamic and circumstances may change. Your plan should be flexible enough to accommodate these changes.

---

* * *

Effectively managing debt requires discipline, planning, and a commitment to financial responsibility. As you make progress in reducing your debt, you free up resources to invest in your future and move closer to financial freedom.

5. CHAPTER INCREASING YOUR INCOME

Boosting your income is a key factor in speeding up your journey to financial freedom. To improve your financial situation, think about ways to earn more, like exploring a side hustle. At the same time, invest any extra money in opportunities that generate income, helping to grow your finances and build wealth over time. Embracing a side hustle can be a proactive way to boost your earnings, while strategic investments can provide avenues for your money to work for you. This dual approach contributes to an overall improvement in your financial situation, paving the way for sustained financial growth.

a. Exploring Side Hustles

Considering side hustles is an excellent way to broaden your income streams, pursue your passions, and accelerate your journey toward financial freedom. At the same time, this could also be an opportunity to explore new skills and interests, potentially turning hobbies into additional sources of income.

Here's A Guide On How To Explore And Start Side Hustles Effectively:

1. Identify Your Skills and Interests

List your skills, hobbies, and interests. This will help you identify potential side hustle opportunities that align with your strengths and passions, turning what you enjoy into a source of additional income.

2. Research Side Hustle Ideas

Explore various side hustle ideas based on your skills and interests. This could include freelancing, consulting, tutoring, writing, graphic design, online selling, and more.

3. Assess Market Demand

Research the market demand for your potential side hustle. Consider the competition, target audience, and potential income. Choose a side hustle that has a viable market.

4. Consider Online Platforms

Explore online platforms that connect freelancers and clients. Websites like Upwork, Fiverr, or Freelancer can be excellent starting points for finding freelance opportunities.

5. Start Small

Begin with a small, manageable side hustle, especially if you have limited time. Starting small allows you to test the waters without overwhelming yourself.

6. Create a Schedule

Develop a schedule that accommodates your side hustle activities. Set realistic goals and allocate dedicated time each week for your side hustle.

7. Build an Online Presence

Create an online presence for your side hustle. This might involve creating a professional website, setting up profiles on social media, or showcasing your work on relevant platforms.

8. Network and Market Yourself

Network with people in your industry and market yourself effectively. Attend networking events, use social media to showcase your skills, and leverage word-of-mouth referrals.

9. Set Financial Goals

Establish clear financial goals for your side hustle. Whether it's to pay off debt, build an emergency fund, or invest, having specific financial objectives can keep you motivated and prevent you from spending this extra income on something less useful and ensure that the additional income from your side hustle is directed toward meaningful goals.

10. Invest in Skill Development

Continuously invest in developing your skills. Take online

courses, attend workshops, and stay updated on industry trends to enhance the value you provide through your side hustle.

11. Legal and Tax Considerations

Be aware of any legal or tax considerations related to your side hustle. Depending on your location and the nature of your work, you may need to register as a freelancer or report additional income on your taxes.

12. Evaluate and Optimize

Regularly evaluate the performance of your side hustle. Assess what's working well and what can be improved. Optimize your strategies to maximize income and efficiency.

13. Diversify Income Streams

Consider diversifying your side hustles to create multiple income streams. This strategy enhances stability and resilience, offering a valuable financial cushion, particularly during periods of economic uncertainty.

14. Balance with Main Job and Personal Life

Maintain a healthy balance between your main job, personal life, and side hustle. Avoid burnout by setting boundaries and ensuring that your side hustle enhances, rather than detracts from your overall well-being.

Additional tips for creating side hustles:

- **Be Patient and Persistent:** Building a successful side hustle takes time. Be patient and stay persistent, especially during the initial stages.
- **Customer Feedback:** Pay attention to customer feedback and reviews. Positive feedback can enhance your reputation and attract more clients.
- **Evaluate Return on Investment (ROI):** Assess the return on investment for your time and effort. Focus on activities that yield the highest ROI.

* * *

Exploring side hustle can be a rewarding venture, providing financial flexibility and the opportunity to pursue your passions. By carefully selecting and managing your side hustle, you can enhance your income and move closer to your financial goals.

b.   Investing in Income-Generating Opportunities

Investing in income-generating opportunities can be a key strategy for building wealth achieving financial freedom and creating a reliable stream of income. By strategically investing in opportunities that generate income, you not only build wealth over time but also pave the way for financial freedom.

Here's A Guide On How To Approach Income-Generating Investments:

1.   Understand Your Financial Goals

Clarify your financial goals before making any investments. Are you looking for regular income to cover living expenses, or are you focused on long-term wealth accumulation? Your investment strategy will be directed by your goals.

2.   Assess Your Risk Tolerance

Evaluate your risk tolerance, as this will influence the types of income-generating investments you choose. Higher-risk investments might offer higher returns, but they come with increased volatility.

3.   Diversify Your Portfolio

Diversification is a crucial concept in investing. Distribute your investments among various types of assets (stocks, bonds, real estate, etc.) and different sectors to lower risk and increase potential returns.

4.   Explore Dividend Stocks

Dividend-paying stocks can be a source of regular income.

Look for companies with a history of stable dividends and a strong financial position.

5. Consider Bonds and Fixed-Income Securities

Bonds and other fixed-income securities are reliable instruments that offer a consistent stream of interest income. Common options include government bonds, municipal bonds, and corporate bonds. These investments provide a stable source of earnings, making them attractive for those seeking a predictable and steady return on their investment.

6. Real Estate Investments

Real estate can generate income through rental payments. You can invest directly in properties or explore real estate investment trusts (REITs), which provide exposure to the real estate market without direct ownership.

7. Peer-to-Peer Lending

Peer-to-peer lending platforms enable you to lend your money in exchange for interest payments, usually to individuals or small businesses. It's a form of fixed-income investment with potentially higher returns than traditional savings accounts.

8. Investment in Dividend ETFs or Mutual Funds

Exchange-traded funds (ETFs) or mutual funds focused on dividend-paying stocks can provide a diversified approach to income investing. They combine money from various investors to invest in a collection of dividends stocks.

9. Preferred Stocks

Preferred stocks are a hybrid between common stocks and bonds. They typically pay higher dividends than common stocks and have a priority claim on company assets.

10. Explore Annuities

Annuities are financial products that provide regular payments over a specified period or for life. They are often used for retirement income.

11. Reinvest Earnings

Reinvesting earnings from income-generating investments can compound returns over time. Consider using dividends or interest payments to acquire more shares or assets.

12. Regularly Review and Adjust

Regularly review your income-generating investments. Economic conditions, interest rates, and market dynamics change, and your portfolio may need adjustments to align with your goals.

13. Tax Efficiency

Be mindful of the tax implications of your investments. Some income sources may be taxed differently than others. Consider tax-efficient investment strategies for your investments. Some income sources may be taxed differently than others.

Additional tips for investing in income-generating opportunities:

- **Stay Informed:** Stay updated on market trends, economic conditions, and fluctuations in interest rates. This knowledge can guide your investment decisions.
- **Consider Professional Advice:** If you're unsure about the best income-generating opportunities for your situation, think about consulting with a financial advisor who can offer tailored guidance based on your specific situation.
- **Emergency Fund First:** Before diving into income-generating investments, ensure you have an adequate emergency fund in place to cover unexpected expenses.

Investing in income-generating opportunities requires a thoughtful and strategic approach. By aligning your investments with your financial goals, considering risk factors, and diversifying your portfolio, you can build a reliable stream of income over time and strengthen your financial position. A thoughtful and strategic approach to investing in income-generating opportunities involves careful alignment with your financial goals.

6. CHAPTER THE BASICS OF INVESTING

Investing involves allocating resources, typically money, with the anticipation of generating a return or profit over time. While the prospect of investing might seem complex or reserved for financial experts, it's an accessible and crucial aspect of financial planning for individuals and businesses alike.

a.   Introduction to Investing

This introduction is geared towards beginners stepping into the world of investing. It covers fundamental concepts to help you grasp the basics of investing strategies, managing risks, and potential returns. Whether you're new to investing or just starting, these key concepts offer a solid foundation for navigating the financial landscape.

The Key Reasons To Invest:

1.   Wealth Growth:

Investing provides an opportunity for your money to grow over time. Instead of keeping funds in a savings account with minimal interest, investments have the potential for higher returns.

2.   Financial Goals:

Investing can help you achieve specific financial goals, whether it's saving for a home, funding education, or building a comfortable retirement nest egg.

3.   Beat Inflation:

Over time, inflation erodes the purchasing power of money. Investing offers a means to potentially outpace inflation and preserve the real value of your wealth.

4.   Diversification:

Diversifying your investments involves spreading your assets across various classes, such as stocks, bonds, real estate, etc. This strategy helps reduce overall risk and enhances the potential for returns.

Basic Investment Types:

1. Stocks:

Ownership: Owning stocks means having ownership in a company. By buying shares, you become a shareholder and own a portion of the company.

Returns: Returns come from capital appreciation (increase in stock price) and dividends (a share of company profits).

2. Bonds:

Lending: A bond is a loan from an investor to a borrower, such as a company or government. The borrower utilizes the funds for its operations, and in return, the investor earns interest on the investment.

Income: Returns come from interest payments, and bonds are considered a lower risk compared to stocks.

3. Mutual Funds:

Pooled Funds: Mutual funds collect money from many investors and subsequently invest in a diversified portfolio of stocks, bonds, or other securities.

Professional Management: They are managed by professionals, offering diversification without the need for individual stock or bond selection.

4. Exchange-Traded Funds (ETFs):

Pooled Funds: Like mutual funds, ETFs gather funds from numerous investors. However, are traded on stock exchanges like individual stocks.

Diversification: ETFs offer diversification and usually have lower fees than many mutual funds.

Additional tips for investing:

- **Risk Tolerance:** Evaluate your risk tolerance, which is your capacity and willingness to withstand fluctuations in the value of your investments. Risk tolerance varies among individuals based on financial goals, time horizon, and personal preferences.
- **Diversification:** Spreading your investments across different assets helps manage risk. A diversified portfolio is less susceptible to the poor performance of a single investment.

How To Get Started:

1. Educate Yourself:

Begin by understanding basic investment principles. Read books, articles, and reputable financial websites to build your knowledge.

2. Define Your Goals:

Clearly define your financial goals and time horizon. Short-term goals might require different investment strategies than long-term goals.

3. Assess Your Risk Tolerance:

Evaluate your risk tolerance honestly. If you're uncomfortable with high volatility, you might lean towards more conservative investments.

4. Create a Budget:

Before investing, establish a budget to ensure you have a precise understanding of your income, expenses, and how much you can allocate to investments.

5. Emergency Fund:

Establish and uphold an emergency fund that covers several months' worth of living expenses. This provides a financial cushion for unexpected events.

6. Start Small:

Begin with a small amount that you can afford to invest. As you gain more confidence and expertise, you can increase your investments.

7. Diversify Your Portfolio:

Diversification is key. Avoid putting all your funds into a single investment. Spread your investments across different asset classes.

8. Review and Adjust:

Regularly review your portfolio and adjust in response to alterations in your financial situation, changes in goals, and changes in the market.

9. Consider Professional Advice:

If you find yourself uncertain about investment decisions, it's worth considering seeking advice from a financial advisor who can offer personalized guidance.

* * *

Investing is a journey that requires time, patience, and continuous learning. By taking a strategic approach and staying informed, you can make well-informed investment choices that support your financial goals.

b. Diversification:

Diversification includes distributing your investments among different types of assets and various asset classes to lower risk and increase the potential for returns. The idea is that a well-diversified portfolio is less susceptible to the poor performance of a single investment.

Key Principles To Diversification:

1. Asset Classes:

Spread your investments across different asset classes, including stocks, bonds, real estate, and commodities, to achieve diversification. Each class reacts differently to economic conditions and market cycles.

2. Geographic Diversification:

Consider investments in different geographic regions. Economic conditions and markets can vary significantly from one country to another, providing additional diversification benefits.

3. Industry Sectors:

Within asset classes, diversify across different industry sectors. For example, instead of investing solely in technology stocks, consider exposure to healthcare, finance, and other sectors.

4. Individual Securities:

Diversify within each asset class by holding a variety of individual securities. Avoid concentrating too much of your portfolio on a single stock or bond.

5. Risk Tolerance:

Align your diversification strategy with your risk tolerance. If you prefer to avoid significant risks, you may incline towards a more conservative combination of assets.

Benefits of diversification:

- **Risk Reduction:** Diversification helps mitigate the impact of poor-performing assets by spreading risk across different investments.
- **Enhanced Returns:** While diversification can't eliminate all risk, it allows you to capture returns from various sources, potentially enhancing overall portfolio performance.
- **Smoothing Volatility:** A diversified portfolio tends to experience fewer extreme fluctuations in value compared to a concentrated one.

---

* * *

It's essential to recognize that diversification is not a one-time task but an ongoing process that should evolve with changes in economic conditions, market trends, and financial goals. Regularly review and rebalance your portfolio to ensure it aligns with your risk tolerance and objectives.

In conclusion, a well-diversified investment portfolio can provide a solid foundation for financial success by managing risk and maximizing potential returns. By carefully spreading your investments across different asset classes, geographic regions, industry sectors, and individual securities, you position yourself to navigate the complexities of the financial markets with greater resilience. Remember that seeking professional advice and staying informed about market dynamics are valuable components of a successful diversification strategy.

c. Risk Management:

Risk management in investing involves identifying, assessing, and mitigating potential risks to protect your portfolio from significant losses. By implementing a comprehensive risk management strategy, you can navigate the uncertainties of the market more effectively, make informed decisions, and safeguard your investment portfolio from significant losses.

Key Principles Of Risk Management:

1. Risk Assessment:

Understand the various types of risks, including credit risk, interest rate risk, market risk, and geopolitical risk. Assess how these risks may impact your investments.

2. Asset Allocation:

Tailor your asset allocation to your financial goals and risk tolerance. This involves deciding what percentage of your portfolio to allocate to different asset classes.

3. Regular Review:

Frequently assess your investment portfolio to make sure it aligns with your risk tolerance and financial objectives. Adjust the portfolio as needed to uphold the desired asset allocation.

4. Emergency Fund:

Maintain an emergency fund separate from your investments. This fund serves as a financial cushion for unexpected expenses and can prevent the need to sell investments during downturns.

5. Dollar-Cost Averaging:

Explore the option of dollar-cost averaging, a regular fixed dollar amount investment, regardless of market conditions. This approach helps minimize the impact of market volatility on your overall investment.

6. Stay Informed:

Keep yourself informed about economic trends, market conditions, and changes in the investment landscape. Awareness allows for timely adjustments to your portfolio.

Benefits for risk management:

- **Preservation of Capital**: Effective risk management aims to protect your capital from significant losses during market downturns.
- **Peace of Mind**: Having a well-thought-out risk management strategy provides peace of mind, allowing you to stay invested with confidence.
- **Adaptability**: A sound risk management approach allows you to adapt to changing market conditions and adjust your portfolio accordingly.

---

* * *

In conclusion, a thriving investment strategy hinges on diversification and effective risk management. Distributing investments across diverse assets, sectors, and geographic regions, coupled with active risk management, creates a robust portfolio aligned with your financial goals. Consistent monitoring and adjustments play a crucial role in sustaining a balanced and effective investment approach.

7. CHAPTER MASTERING THE ART OF SAVING

Mastering the art of saving is a vital skill in today's dynamic financial landscape. It goes beyond merely setting money aside; it involves strategic decision-making, preparing for the unexpected, and working toward long-term financial goals. Savings you're building an emergency fund or investing in the future, the art of saving provides the foundation for financial stability and prosperity.

a.   Saving Techniques

Saving money is a fundamental financial habit that forms the foundation for achieving financial goals and accumulating wealth.

The Following Are Saving Techniques To Assist In Managing Your Money Wisely:

1.   Create a Budget

Importance: A budget is a roadmap for your finances, providing clarity on income, expenses, and savings goals.

Tips: Categorize expenses, allocate funds for savings, and track your spending against the budget regularly.

2.   Pay Yourself First

Importance: Prioritize savings by setting aside a portion of your income before spending it on other expenses.

Tips: Automate transfers to a savings account or investment account immediately after receiving your paycheck.

3.   Emergency Fund

Importance: An emergency fund is important as a financial safety net for unforeseen expenses or emergencies

Tips: Strive to save an amount equivalent to three to six months' worth of living expenses in a liquid and easily accessible account.

4.   Track and Analyze Expenses

Importance: Knowing where your money is spent is essential for pinpointing areas where you can reduce expenses and save.

Tips: Use budgeting apps or tools to categorize and analyze your spending patterns.

5. Cut Unnecessary Expenses

Importance: Eliminating non-essential expenses frees up more money for saving and investing.

Tips: Identify discretionary spending areas, such as dining out or subscription services, and find ways to reduce or eliminate them.

6. Set Specific Savings Goals

Importance: Having clear savings goals gives you motivation and a purpose for saving.

Tips: Define short-term and long-term goals, for example, a vacation, home purchase, or retirement. Allocate funds specifically for each goal.

7. Automate Savings

Importance: Automation ensures consistent savings without relying on willpower.

Tips: Set up automatic transfers to savings or investment accounts. Many employers also allow direct deposit into multiple accounts.

8. Take Advantage of Employer Benefits

Importance: Employer benefits can include retirement plans, health savings accounts (HSAs), or other perks.

Tips: Contribute to employer-sponsored retirement plans and take advantage of any matching contributions. Use HSAs for healthcare expenses.

9. Shop Smarter

Importance: Being mindful of your spending habits helps you save on everyday purchases.

Tips: Look for discounts, use coupons, and compare prices before making purchases. Consider buying generic brands and avoiding impulse buys.

10. Review and Negotiate Bills

Importance: Regularly reviewing bills can identify opportunities to reduce costs.

Tips: Negotiate with service providers for better rates, cancel unused subscriptions, and explore options for reducing utility bills.

11. Use Cash Envelopes

Importance: Cash envelopes help control spending in specific categories.

Tips: Allocate a fixed amount of cash for discretionary spending categories like groceries or entertainment. When the cash is gone, stop spending in that category.

12. Sell Unneeded Items

Importance: Decluttering can be a source of extra income.

Tips: Sell items you no longer need through online platforms, garage sales, or consignment stores.

13. Participate in Savings Challenges

Importance: Savings challenges add an element of fun and motivation to the saving process.

Tips: Join savings challenges, such as the 52-week savings challenge or monthly savings challenges. Adjust the challenge to fit your budget.

14. Refinance Debts

Importance: Refinancing high-interest debts can lower monthly payments and free up funds for saving.

Tips: Explore refinancing options for loans with high interest rates, such as credit cards or student loans.

15. Buy Used and Prioritize Value

Value: Opting for used items and prioritizing value is a savvy financial choice that allows you to stretch your budget, minimize depreciation impact on your wallet, and make environmentally conscious decisions.

Tips: Prioritize value by conducting thorough research, inspecting, and testing products, buying from reputable sellers, considering certified pre-owned options for significant purchases, negotiating prices, and focusing on overall value rather than brand names.

Additional tips on saving:

- **Regularly Reevaluate Expenses:** Periodically review your budget and expenses to identify new opportunities for saving.
- **Celebrate Milestones:** Celebrate savings milestones to stay motivated. Acknowledge achievements, whether big or small, as you progress toward your goals.
- **Stay Consistent:** Saving is a habit that develops over time. Consistency is key, even if you start with small amounts.

---

* * *

By adopting these saving techniques and incorporating them into your financial routine, you can build a strong foundation for financial stability and work towards achieving your short-term and long-term financial goals.

b.   Overcoming Common Savings Challenges

Saving money can be challenging, especially in the face of everyday expenses, unexpected emergencies, and the temptation to indulge in immediate pleasures.

Here Are Strategies To Overcome Common Savings Challenges:

1.   Challenge: Limited Income

Strategy: Focus on Essentials

Prioritize necessary expenses like rent, utilities, and groceries. Create a budget that allocates a percentage of your income to savings, no matter how small.

Strategy: Increase Income

Explore ways to increase your income, like taking on freelance work, a part-time job, or a side hustle. Consider acquiring new skills that can lead to higher-paying opportunities.

2. Challenge: High Expenses

Strategy: Trim Unnecessary Spending

Identify discretionary spending areas and cut back where possible. This could include dining out less often, cancelling unnecessary subscriptions, prioritising sustainability, or finding more cost-effective alternatives.

Strategy: Negotiate Bills

Negotiate with service providers for better rates on bills. This applies to utilities, insurance, and even credit card interest rates. Many providers are willing to work with customers who ask for discounts.

3. Challenge: Lack of Emergency Fund

Strategy: Start Small

If building an emergency fund seems overwhelming, start with small, regular contributions. Gradually increase the amount as your financial situation improves.

Strategy: Allocate Windfalls

Use unexpected windfalls, such as tax refunds or bonuses, to kickstart or boost your emergency fund.

4. Challenge: Debt Repayment

Strategy: Prioritize Lowest Balance or Highest-Interest Debt

Decide if you start paying off debts with the lowest balance or the highest interest rates first. Paying the lowest balance could be more motivating since you see the result sooner but paying the highest interest debt first will save you money in the long run.

Strategy: Consolidate Debt

Explore options for consolidating high-interest debt into a lower-interest loan or credit card. This can make repayment more manageable.

5. Challenge: Lack of Discipline

Strategy: Automate Savings

Set up automatic transfers to your savings account to ensure that a portion of your income is saved before you have the chance to spend it.

Strategy: Use Behavioral Tricks

Trick your brain into saving by treating it as a bill. Create a "savings bill" in your budget and treat it with the same level of importance as your rent or mortgage payment.

6. Challenge: Short-Term Focus

Strategy: Set Clear Goals

Define specific, achievable savings goals. Whether it's an emergency fund, a vacation, or a down payment on a home, having a clear goal provides motivation.

Strategy: Visualize Future Benefits

Visualize the long-term benefits of saving. Consider the financial security, freedom, and opportunities that come with disciplined saving.

7. Challenge: Financial Literacy Gap

Strategy: Educate Yourself

Increase your financial literacy by reading books, attending workshops, or taking online courses. Understanding the principles of personal finance can empower you to make well-informed decisions.

Strategy: Consider consulting with a professional for

advice

Consult with a financial advisor for personalized guidance. Professionals can assist you in navigating intricate financial scenarios and customizing strategies to suit your individual needs.

8. Challenge: Lack of Accountability

Strategy: Share Goals with a Partner or Friend

Having an accountability partner can make the savings journey more enjoyable and effective. Share your goals with a friend or family member who can offer support and encouragement.

Strategy: Track Progress Regularly

Regularly review your savings progress. Use tools like apps or spreadsheets to monitor your success and adjust your strategies as needed.

9. Challenge: Economic Uncertainty

Stragety: Build Resilience

Focus on building financial resilience by having an emergency fund, reducing debt, and diversifying income sources. These measures can help you weather economic uncertainties more effectively.

Strategy: Stay Informed

Stay informed about economic trends and potential challenges. Awareness allows for proactive adjustments to your financial strategies.

10. Challenge: Lack of Motivation

Strategy: Visualize Success

Create a vision board or a written description of the financial future you aspire to. Visualizing success can reignite motivation during challenging times.

Strategy: Reward Yourself

Celebrate milestones along the way. Treat yourself to a small reward when you reach savings goals to reinforce positive behaviour.

Additional tips for saving challenges:

- **Stay Flexible**: Life is dynamic and so the circumstances and your financial plan may need to be adapted accordingly. Be flexible and willing to adapt your savings strategies as needed.
- **Celebrate Progress**: Celebrate small victories and progress on your savings journey. Positive reinforcement can enhance motivation.
- **Seek Support**: If you're struggling with saving, consider joining online communities or forums where individuals share tips and experiences. Supportive communities can provide encouragement and practical advice.

✳ ✳ ✳

Overcoming savings challenges requires a combination of discipline, strategic planning, and adaptability. By employing these strategies and staying committed to your financial goals, you can build a solid foundation for a more secure and financially prosperous future.

8. CHAPTER MINDSET SHIFTS FOR FINANCIAL SUCCESS

Explore the transformative power of shifting your perspective on money and abundance and discover the key principles that will empower you to make informed financial decisions and instil the discipline needed for lasting financial success. To achieve prosperity, it's crucial not just to comprehend the mindset shifts required for wealth creation but also to apply the practices that nurture financial discipline throughout your journey.

a. Cultivating a Wealth Mindset

Cultivating a wealth mindset involves adopting a set of beliefs and attitudes that promote financial abundance, success, and a positive relationship with money.

Here Are Key Principles To Help You Develop A Wealth Mindset:

1. Believe in Abundance

Shift from Scarcity to Abundance: Replace thoughts of scarcity with those of abundance. Believe that there are ample opportunities, resources, and wealth to go around.

Avoid a Zero-Sum Mentality: Reject the idea that someone else's success means less for you. The economy and opportunities are not fixed; there is room for everyone to thrive.

2. Embrace a Growth Mindset

See Challenges as Opportunities: View challenges and setbacks as opportunities for growth and learning. A growth mindset sees effort and perseverance as the path to mastery.

Continuous Learning: Cultivate a love for learning. Stay curious, seek new knowledge, and be open to acquiring new skills that can contribute to your financial success.

3. Focus on Solutions, Not Problems

Positive Problem-Solving: Instead of dwelling on problems, focus on finding solutions. A wealth mindset sees challenges as temporary roadblocks that can be overcome.

Opportunities in Adversity: Look for opportunities even in difficult situations. Adversity can be a catalyst for innovation and growth.

4. Take Calculated Risks

Risk-Taking as a Growth Strategy: Embrace calculated risks as part of the wealth-building process. Understand that taking risks, when well-researched and managed, can lead to substantial rewards.

Learn from Failure: See failure as a stepping stone to success. Analyze what went wrong, learn from it, use that knowledge to improve future decisions and view failure as a stepping stone to success. Embracing failure as a learning opportunity is a key element in the journey toward ultimate success.

5. Visualize Success

Create a Clear Vision: Develop a clear vision of your financial goals and success. Visualization can help program your mind for success and keep you motivated.

Use Affirmations: Repeat positive affirmations related to wealth and success. Affirmations can reinforce positive beliefs and reshape your subconscious mind instilling a positive mindset towards wealth and success. Consistently repeating affirmations has the power to strengthen positive beliefs, reshape your subconscious mind, and foster a mindset conducive to achieving financial success.

6. Build a Network of Success-Oriented Individuals

Surround Yourself with Positivity: Associate with people who have a positive mindset about wealth and success. Their mindset can influence your thinking and outlook on life.

Learn from Mentors: Seek guidance from mentors who have achieved financial success. Learn from their experiences, insights, and advice. Leverage their wisdom to navigate your own path to financial success. By seeking guidance from mentors who have achieved financial prosperity, you can glean valuable insights, learn from their experiences, and apply their advice to your own journey toward financial well-being.

7. Invest in Yourself

Continuous Self-Improvement: Invest in your education, skills, and personal development. The more you invest in yourself, the more value you can contribute to others and the world.

Prioritize Health and Well-Being: Physical and mental well-being are essential for sustained success. Take care of your health as it directly impacts your ability to pursue and enjoy wealth.

8. Celebrate Success, Big and Small

Acknowledge Achievements: Celebrate your successes, whether they are major milestones or small wins. Acknowledging your achievements reinforces a positive mindset.

Gratitude Practices: Cultivate gratitude for what you have achieved and the opportunities that come your way. Gratitude attracts more positive experiences.

9. Create Multiple Income Streams

Diversify Income Sources: Embrace the idea of having multiple income streams. This not only provides financial security but also aligns with the wealthy mindset of creating abundance.

Explore Entrepreneurship: Consider entrepreneurial ventures or side businesses. Entrepreneurship is often driven by a mindset that sees opportunities where others see challenges.

10. Give Back and Contribute

Philanthropy and Contribution: Contribute to causes you believe in. A wealth mindset includes the understanding that true wealth involves making a positive impact on the world.

Generosity Mindset: Embrace a mindset of generosity. Share your knowledge, resources, and success with others, fostering a cycle of abundance.

Additional tips for a wealth mind shift:

- **Monitor Your Language:** Pay attention to the language you use when talking about money and success. The shift from negative or limiting language to positive, empowering expressions.

- **Stay Persistent:** Developing a wealth mindset is a journey that requires persistence. Be patient with yourself and consistently reinforce positive beliefs and habits.

- **Reflect Regularly:** Regularly reflect on your beliefs and attitudes toward money. Identify and challenge any negative or limiting thoughts that may arise.

- **Align Actions with Mindset:** Ensure that your actions align with your wealth mindset. Consistent actions based on positive beliefs reinforce the mindset over time.

---

* * *

Cultivating a wealth mindset is about adopting a positive and proactive approach to financial success. By embracing abundance, staying open to growth, and consistently reinforcing positive beliefs, you can create a mindset that sets the stage for long-term wealth and fulfilment.

b.   Developing Financial Discipline

Building financial discipline is essential for reaching long-term financial goals and sustaining a healthy financial well-being.

Here Are Practical Strategies To Help You Cultivate And Enhance Financial Discipline:

1.   Set Clear Financial Goals

Define specific, measurable, and time-bound financial goals. Having clear objectives provides direction and motivation for disciplined financial behaviour.

2.   Create a Realistic Budget

Create a thorough budget that details your income, expenses, and savings goals. Allocate funds for necessities, discretionary spending, and savings in a way that aligns with your goals.

3.   Prioritize Saving

Make saving a non-negotiable part of your budget. Consider it an expense that you pay yourself. Set up automatic transfers to your savings or investment accounts to ensure consistency.

4.   Emergency Fund

Establish and maintain an emergency fund. Strive to accumulate three to six months' worth of living expenses in an easily accessible account to address unforeseen expenses.

5.   Avoid Impulse Spending

Practice mindful spending by avoiding impulsive

purchases. Before making a non-essential purchase, ask yourself if it aligns with your financial goals and if you genuinely need it.

6. Distinguish Between Needs and Wants

Differentiate between essential needs and discretionary wants. Prioritize spending on needs first and allocate the remaining funds to wants based on your financial goals.

7. Limit the Use of Credit

Use credit cards judiciously and avoid accumulating high-interest debt. Pay off credit card balances in full each month to prevent interest charges from eroding your financial discipline.

8. Track Your Expenses

Regularly monitor and review your spending to ensure it aligns with your budget. Utilize budgeting apps or tools to track expenses and identify areas for improvement.

9. Establish Financial Routines

Set specific routines for managing your finances, such as reviewing your budget weekly, tracking expenses daily, or reviewing your financial goals monthly.

10. Automate Finances

Set up automatic transfers for bill payments, savings, and investments. Automation ensures that financial responsibilities are met consistently and reduces the chance of oversights.

11. Accountability

Share your financial goals and progress with a trusted

friend, family member, or financial advisor. Having someone to hold you accountable can enhance your commitment to financial discipline.

12. Regularly Review and Adjust

Regularly revisit your budget and financial goals. Adjust them as needed based on changes in your income, expenses, or life circumstances.

13. Practice Delayed Gratification

Develop the habit of delaying immediate gratification for long-term benefits. This applies to both spending decisions and lifestyle choices that may impact your finances.

14. Educate Yourself

Invest time in increasing your financial literacy. Grasping the principles of personal finance gives you the ability to make informed decisions and strengthens your discipline in managing finances.

15. Celebrate Financial Milestones

Acknowledge and celebrate milestones along your financial journey. Recognizing achievements, whether big or small, provides positive reinforcement.

16. Create a Debt Repayment Plan

For all outstanding debts, develop a structured repayment plan. Prioritize high-interest debts while making consistent payments on others.

17. Live Below Your Means

Adopt a lifestyle that allows you to live comfortably below your means. This creates room for savings and provides a financial cushion.

18. Practice Contentment

Cultivate contentment and gratitude for what you have. A mindset of contentment reduces the desire for unnecessary consumption and supports financial discipline.

19. Emergency Preparedness

Develop plans for handling financial emergencies. This may involve having insurance coverage, an emergency fund, and contingency plans for unexpected events.

20. Seek Professional Advice

Consult with financial advisors or experts when needed. Experts can offer tailored advice according to your specific circumstances and financial objectives.

Additional tips for financial discipline:

- **Stay Disciplined During Windfalls**: Whether it's a tax refund, bonus, or unexpected income, stay disciplined by allocating a portion to savings or debt repayment.
- **Regularly Assess Financial Health:** Periodically evaluate your overall financial health, including net worth, debt-to-income ratio, and progress toward financial goals.
- **Review and Optimize Bills**: Regularly review your recurring bills to identify opportunities for cost savings. Negotiate with service providers and explore alternative options.
- **Cultivate a Long-Term Perspective**: Developing financial discipline is about making choices that align with your long-term goals. Keep the big picture in mind when facing daily financial decisions.
- **Learn from Mistakes:** If you make financial mistakes or deviate from your plan, use them as learning opportunities. Identify the cause and adjust to prevent similar occurrences in the future.

* * *

Cultivating financial discipline is an ongoing process that requires commitment, self-awareness, and strategic planning. By integrating these principles into your financial habits, you can build a strong foundation for achieving your financial objectives and maintaining a healthy financial life.

9. CHAPTER SUSTAINING FINANCIAL FREEDOM

As we delve into the nuances of sustaining financial freedom, this chapter unfolds three pivotal aspects: monitoring and adjusting your plan, adapting to economic changes, and the transformative power of inspiring others and giving back. Together, these elements form the cornerstone of a resilient and enduring financial journey.

a.   Monitoring and Adjusting Your Plan

Regularly reviewing and adjusting your financial plan is a vital aspect of sustaining financial well-being and adapting to changing circumstances.

Here Are Key Steps To Effectively Monitor And Adjust Your Financial Plan:

1.   Regularly Review Your Budget

Frequency: Conduct a thorough review of your budget at least monthly.

Action Steps:
- Compare actual spending to your budgeted amounts.
- Identify any variances and understand the reasons behind them.
- Adjust future budgets based on insights gained from the review.

2.   Track Your Net Worth

Frequency: Review your net worth at least quarterly.

Action Steps:
- Calculate your assets and liabilities.
- Assess changes in your net worth over time.
- Identify areas for improvement, such as reducing debt or increasing savings.

3.   Evaluate and Adjust Financial Goals

Frequency: Reassess your financial goals annually or when major life changes occur.

Action Steps:
- Review the progress toward your financial goals.

- Adjust goals based on changes in income, expenses, or priorities.
- Set new goals or modify existing ones to reflect evolving circumstances.

4. Monitor and Manage Debt

Frequency: Regularly review your outstanding debts.

Action Steps:
- Track the progress of debt repayment.
- Consider refinancing or consolidating high-interest debts.
- Adjust debt repayment strategies based on changes in financial circumstances.

5. Review Investment Portfolios

Frequency: Periodically assess your investment portfolio, at least annually.

Action Steps:
- Evaluate the performance of your investments.
- Adjust the composition of your portfolio to ensure it aligns with your preferred asset allocation. Consider adjusting your investment strategy based on changes in financial goals or market conditions.

6. Assess Emergency Fund Adequacy

Frequency: Review your emergency fund periodically.

Action Steps:
- Assess whether your emergency fund is sufficient for current circumstances.
- Adjust the fund size based on changes in income, expenses, or financial responsibilities.

7. Reevaluate Insurance Coverage

Frequency: Review insurance policies annually or when major life changes occur.

Action Steps:
- Ensure that your insurance coverage aligns with your current needs.
- Consider adjusting coverage based on changes in family size, income, or assets.

8. Adjust Tax Planning

Frequency: Conduct a tax review annually, especially as tax laws change.

Action Steps:
- Optimize your tax strategy based on changes in income and deductions.
- Explore tax-efficient investment options.
- Leverage available tax credits and deductions.

9. Evaluate and Adjust Spending Habits

Frequency: Regularly assess your spending habits.

Action Steps:
- Identify areas where you can cut discretionary spending.
- Reevaluate subscriptions and recurring expenses.
- Redirect savings from reduced spending toward financial goals.

10. Review and Update Legal Documents

Frequency: Review legal documents as needed or at least annually.

Action Steps:
- Ensure that wills, trusts, and other legal documents

reflect your current wishes.
- Update beneficiaries on accounts and insurance policies.
- Consult with legal professionals for guidance on estate planning.

11. Monitor Credit Reports

Frequency: Review your credit report at least annually.

Action Steps:
- Check for inaccuracies or suspicious activities.
- Address any issues promptly to maintain a healthy credit profile.

12. Stay Informed About Economic Trends

Frequency: Regularly stay informed about economic trends and financial news.

Action Steps:
- Understand how economic conditions may impact on your finances.
- Adjust your financial plan based on changing economic circumstances.

13. Seek Professional Guidance

Frequency: Consult with financial advisors periodically or when facing complex financial decisions.

Action Steps:
- Seek advice on investment strategies, tax planning, and overall financial planning.
- Utilize professional guidance to navigate specific financial challenges.

Additional tips for adjusting your plan:

- **Document Changes**: Keep a record of changes made to your financial plan, including the reasons for adjustments and the expected outcomes.
- **Emergency Plan Updates**: Ensure that your emergency plans, such as evacuation plans or crisis preparedness, are regularly reviewed and updated.
- **Stay Adaptable:** Be open to adjusting your financial plan as needed. Life is dynamic, and your financial plan should evolve to meet changing circumstances.
- **Review Insurances for Life Changes**: Whenever you experience significant life changes (marriage, children, job changes), review your insurance coverage to ensure it adequately protects your new circumstances.
- **Celebrate Achievements**: Celebrate financial milestones and achievements. Recognizing progress boosts motivation and reinforces positive financial habits.

* * *

Monitoring and adjusting your financial plan are not a one-time task but an ongoing process. Regular reviews, adjustments, and staying informed about changes in your financial landscape are essential for maintaining financial health and working towards your long-term goals.

b.   Adapting to Economic Changes

Adapting to economic changes is a crucial skill for financial well-being. Economic conditions can fluctuate, affecting employment, investments, and overall financial stability.

Here Are Strategies To Help You Adapt To Economic Changes:

1.   Build a Robust Emergency Fund

Importance: An emergency fund provides a financial cushion during economic uncertainties.

Action Steps:
- Ensure your emergency fund is well-funded.
- Adjust your emergency fund size based on economic conditions and potential job market volatility.

2.   Diversify Your Income Sources

Importance: Dependence on a single income source can increase vulnerability.

Action Steps:
- Explore side hustle, freelance opportunities, or part-time work.
- Diversify investments to include a range of asset classes.

3.   Reassess and Adjust the Budget

Importance: Economic changes can impact income and expenses.

Action Steps:
- Regularly assess and modify your budget to match shifts in income or expenses.

- Prioritize essential expenses and cut back on non-essential spending.

4. Evaluate and Strengthen Job Skills

Importance: Economic shifts may impact job markets and demand for specific skills.

Action Steps:
- Stay informed about industry trends.
- Invest in ongoing education and skill development to remain competitive.

5. Stay Informed About Economic Trends

Importance: Awareness of economic conditions allows for proactive planning.

Action Steps:
- Regularly follow economic news and updates.
- Stay informed about industry-specific trends and changes.

6. Review and Adjust Investments

Importance: Economic fluctuations can impact investment values.

Action Steps:
- Periodically review your investment portfolio.
- Adjust your asset allocation based on economic conditions and your risk tolerance.

7. Manage Debt Wisely

Importance: High debt levels can be a financial burden during economic downturns.

Action Steps:
- Prioritize paying down high-interest debt.

- Refinance or consolidate debts if it makes financial sense.

8. Explore Additional Income Streams

Importance: Multiple income streams provide financial resilience.

Action Steps:
- Identify opportunities for additional income, such as a side business or investments.
- Consider passive income streams like dividends or rental income.

9. Reevaluate Long-Term Financial Goals

Importance: Economic changes may impact the feasibility of certain goals.

Action Steps:
- Review your long-term financial goals.
- Adjust timelines or set new goals based on current economic conditions.

10. Stay Conservative in Financial Decisions

Importance: Prudent financial decisions mitigate risks during economic uncertainty.

Action Steps:
- Be conservative in major financial decisions.
- Avoid making large financial commitments without careful consideration.

11. Network and Build Professional Relationships

Importance: Professional connections can provide support during economic challenges.

Action Steps:

- Network within your industry and community.
- Build relationships that may lead to job opportunities or collaborations.

12. Adapt to Remote Work Opportunities

Importance: Remote work can offer flexibility and opportunities during economic changes.

Action Steps:
- Enhance remote work skills and familiarity with relevant tools.
- Explore remote work options within your current job or seek remote opportunities in your field.

13. Reassess Insurance Coverage

Importance: Adequate insurance protects against unexpected events.

Action Steps:
Review and update insurance coverage, including health, life, and property.
Consider additional coverage based on changing circumstances.

14. Explore Government Assistance Programs

Importance: During economic downturns, government assistance programs may be available.

Action Steps:
- Stay informed about available assistance programs.
- Evaluate eligibility and apply for relevant programs when needed.

15. Seek Professional Advice

Importance: Financial advisors can provide guidance

tailored to your unique circumstances.

Action Steps:
- Consult with financial professionals during significant economic changes.
- Get advice on investment strategies, debt management, and overall financial planning.

Additional tips for adapting to economic changes:

- **Stay Flexible:** Flexibility is key during economic changes. Be open to adjusting your plans as needed.
- **Crisis Preparedness:** Develop a crisis preparedness plan that includes financial considerations, such as job loss or economic downturns.
- **Continuous Learning:** Stay proactive in learning about personal finance and economic trends. A continuous learning mindset positions you to adapt more effectively.
- **Focus on Financial Health:** Prioritize financial health over short-term gains. Long-term financial stability is often the result of prudent and sustainable financial practices.

✳ ✳ ✳

Adapting to economic changes requires a combination of proactive planning, financial resilience, and a willingness to adjust strategies as needed. By implementing these strategies, you can navigate economic uncertainties more effectively and maintain a secure financial foundation.

c.   Inspiring Others and Giving Back

Promoting financial freedom, inspiring others, and giving back can create a positive cycle of empowerment and community building.

Here's A Comprehensive Approach That Combines These Elements:

1.   Financial Freedom Workshops

Host workshops or webinars to educate others about the principles of financial freedom. Share strategies for budgeting, investing, and debt management.

2.   Mentorship Programs

Establish mentorship programs where individuals can receive guidance on their journey to financial freedom. Experienced individuals can mentor those seeking financial advice.

3.   Community Investment Clubs

Create investment clubs within your community where members pool resources to invest collectively. This not only promotes financial education but also allows for shared financial gains.

4.   Financial Literacy Initiatives

Launch initiatives to improve financial literacy in schools and community centres. Work with local educators to integrate practical financial education into the curriculum.

5.   Community Resource Centers

Establish community resource centres that offer free financial counselling, workshops, and resources. Make these centres accessible to individuals seeking guidance on their financial journey.

6. Scholarships for Financial Education

Offer scholarships for individuals to attend financial education courses, workshops, or conferences. This can encourage continuous learning and skill development.

7. Inspiration Through Personal Stories

Share personal stories of financial transformation. Highlight individuals or families who have achieved financial freedom and how they did it. Personal narratives can inspire and provide practical insights.

8. Giving Back Initiatives

Channel a portion of financial gains into community initiatives. This could involve sponsoring local projects, supporting education, or contributing to charitable causes.

9. Financial Freedom Challenges

Organize challenges within your community that encourage people to set and achieve financial goals. Celebrate the achievements of participants and share their success stories.

10. Collaborate with Nonprofits

Partner with nonprofit organizations that focus on financial literacy and empowerment. Contribute resources, time, or expertise to support their initiatives.

11. Philanthropic Investment

Use investment returns to fund philanthropic projects. This approach aligns financial success with social impact, creating a model where financial freedom benefits the community.

12. Community Investment Funds

Establish community investment funds that individuals can contribute to voluntarily. These funds can then be used for community development projects or emergency assistance.

13. Financial Freedom Podcasts or Blogs

Create a podcast or blog that shares insights into achieving financial freedom. Feature interviews with experts and success stories to inspire a broader audience.

14. Financial Wellness Events

Organize events focused on financial wellness, bringing together experts, motivational speakers, and community members. Include workshops and interactive sessions to engage participants.

15. Partnerships with Local Businesses

Partner with local businesses to sponsor financial literacy events or workshops. This collaboration can benefit both the community and businesses.

16. Investing in Local Entrepreneurs

Provide support and investment to local entrepreneurs looking to start or expand businesses. This can contribute to economic development and job creation.

17. Community Crowdfunding Initiatives

Launch crowdfunding campaigns for community projects or individuals in need. This fosters a sense of collective responsibility and support.

18. Financial Freedom Challenges for Charity

Organize fundraising challenges tied to financial goals. For example, participants can commit to saving a certain amount, and funds raised go to a charitable cause.

19. Financial Freedom for Youth

Develop age-appropriate financial literacy programs for youth. Instilling financial knowledge early empowers the next generation towards financial independence.

20. Collaborate with Financial Institutions

Partner with banks or financial institutions to offer community-specific financial education programs, workshops, or access to financial resources.

Additional tips for inspiring and giving back:

- **Celebrate Milestones:** Acknowledge and celebrate the financial milestones of individuals within the community. Recognition can motivate others to pursue their financial goals.
- **Create a Supportive Community:** Foster a sense of community where individuals feel supported and encouraged in their financial journeys. Peer support is a powerful motivator.
- **Feedback and Improvement:** Gather feedback from participants in financial programs to continually improve and tailor initiatives to the needs of the community.
- **Promote Inclusivity:** Ensure that financial education and empowerment initiatives are inclusive and accessible to individuals of diverse backgrounds, socioeconomic statuses, and ages.

* * *

By intertwining financial freedom, inspiration, and giving back, you create a holistic approach to community development. This model not only encourages individual financial empowerment but also contributes to the overall well-being and prosperity of the community.

AFTERWORD

Embrace the journey, wield your newfound knowledge, and may your pursuit of financial freedom be the gateway to a life of abundance, security, and fulfilment.

BB MYRDAL